The Journeyman

A biographical insight into one man's trek through the martial arts.

By Bob Sykes

The Journeyman
By Bob Sykes

Typeset and Design by DK Print Ltd
Publisher: Fiaz Rafiq

ISBN:0955264804
Published by HNL Publishing: A division of HNL Media Group.
E Mail: hnlpub@hotmail.com

Disclaimer - Neither the author nor the publisher assumes any responsibility in any manner whatsoever for any injury which may occur by reading or following the instructions herein.

Consult your physician before following any of the activities.

The Journeyman

By Bob Sykes

The Pen and I

The pen and I good friends at last,

After the bitterness of the past,

In harmony now,

perhaps we can grow,

Sweeter Fruit,

From words we sow.

Dave Smith 2002

This book is dedicated to Vernon Dore.
Unsung hero of the Martial Arts.

Acknowledgements

Martial Arts Illustrated Magazine - Martialartsltd@btconnect.com

A Shotokan Karate Book of Dates.
By Clive Layten and Michael Randall.

Steve Rowe Shikon Martial Arts

Photographers:
Paul Rayner
Jackie Jessop

Contents

Introduction — 9

Karate Years pt1 — 10

Chinto Kata — 18

Karate Years pt2 — 28

Techniques of Karate — 32

The Freestyle Years — 44

Techniques of Freestyle — 50

The Kickboxing Years — 56

Techniques of Kickboxing — 64

The Wing Chun Wars — 68

When Bob met Bill — 76

The Warriors — 80

The Stick Years — 88

Techniques of Eskrima — 96

The Learning Never Stops — 112

What about Bob — 117

A special thankyou for those who helped along the way — 122

Introduction *by Karl Tanswell ~ Straight Blast UK*

Imagine for a moment the type of person who asked me to write the introduction to their book…. EXACTLY!!

I thought it was a wind up. Here we go again, Bob Sykes setting me up. Bob rarely takes anybody seriously least of all himself. When he told me he was going to write a book for fun I was dubious. I have spent years in conversation with martial arts people and have lost count of the times that I have been told they are writing a book.

The desire to develop a product range I can only guess is to reaffirm their status within the "flea circus." If the task of a book ever materialises the content is usually lame self-promotion combined with recycled drivel.

Not to be a negative every so often a gem appears is in the case with this book. I have listened to these stories for years, but never with the background and depth these pages contain. As always there are many different layers on which these stories can be understood. In these pages Bobs true dynamic quality shines through as the oracle guides you through the ridiculousness of the martial arts matrix.

It is very difficult to say anything really genuine about Bob and make it believable.

Bob has been there, done that and doesn't always wear the T-shirt, hooded top or jogging pants to prove it! If you stripped the many masks away from his public persona you will find the archetypal jester and ultimate guide.

I have watched Bob assist many people along their path (always non-judgmentally?) and with non-concern for his own gain (well nearly always).

I am honoured to have Bob as a friend and even more thankful that I was one of his pet projects.

Bob and the martial arts would have to be a parallel with Jack Nicholson and "One Flew Over the Cuckoo's Nest" Like they say,

" in a court of kings usually only the jester knows what's really going on".

Karl Tanswell (centre) with a few famous faces at the Colne Valley Black Belt Academy.

The Karate Years

It was Jubilee year, 1977, when I first tried on a Karate Gi in order to take part in and practise the art of Wado Ryu Karate. Not unlike many who take up the martial arts, I'd previously been interested for a long time, reading the odd Karate manual and viewing the occasional episode of the (then popular) TV series, **Kung Fu**. I even recalled a news snippet referencing the Great Britain Karate Squad that, in 1976, beat Japan and became World Champions ~ more about that later.

A school pal of mine talked me into training at a local Karate club, located about four miles west of Huddersfield in Slaithwaite. Slaithwaite is situated in the Colne Valley, which borders the very hilly and rugged Pennines. For those who want to build up a mental picture, just try watching 'Last of the Summer Wine' or 'Where the Heart Is' as the Colne Valley provides locations for both programmes. Anyway, enough of the where, let's get back to the when.

It was a time when people's enthusiasm was still feeding off Bruce Lee's films and the Kung Fu boom. One major benefit of living in the North of England is that every fad or gimmick seems to catch on a couple of years later than everywhere else (with the exception of cultural music). This gave me the opportunity to get involved and experience the tail end of the Kung Fu boom a couple of years before the bubble finally burst. It was an era of innocence when untainted Karate Kas punched from the heart as well as the hip (or at least that's how it appeared to me). Tournament fighters such as Lau Gar's Steve Babbs and Shotokan's Terry O'Neil were as good as 'Top of the Pops' as they were literally household names within the realm of British martial arts. However, it all appeared, to my friends and family at the time, to be some sort of strange sub culture or occult activity. This was mainly due to the fact that, back then, good Karate, Kung Fu and the newly introduced tae Kwon Do had virtually no PR machine, the only real edifying sources being the television or cinema screen. No cable networks, Sky, or satellite channels, not even the Internet.

Master Sakagami of Wado Ryu Karate

By 1980 I was well and truly bitten by the Karate bug.

It's little wonder that public perception arrived at so many crack-brained solutions. My hat goes off to the Judo fraternity who did a very good job of distancing themselves from it all. They were, and still are, an Olympic sport and took a much more direct and healthy approach when Brian Jacks became a bit of a TV celebrity after winning the prime time TV series 'Superstars'. For those of us who can remember the days before Sky TV - when the entire population thought three channels were ample just about everyone tuned in to watch 'Superstars'. And guess what? This Judo guy, Brian Jacks, a superb athlete and martial artist (who, up until then was virtually unknown outside the Olympic sport of Judo) took on and beat a whole host of personalities from much better known sporting arenas. In the process, Jacks became a tremendous advert for British Judo.

World Karate Champion Victor Charles was later to follow in Jack's footsteps and, while flying the flag for Karate, he laid waste to all other athletes on the programme. As a result, Karate was forced out of the novelty shops and became a socially acceptable activity. Prior to this, the only valid publicity came in 1976 when the British Karate Squad, with its legendary line up of Ticky Donovan of Ishin Ryu, Shotokan's Billy Higgins and Terry O'Neil, Shukokai's Stan Knighten and Billy Fitkin, were victorious against Japan in the finals to become the World Karate champions. To my reckoning this was the most recognisable Karate team ever to represent our island and, as I've already mentioned, the publicity was huge. Sadly it was short lived and it wasn't too long before the British media appeared to once again distance itself from the martial arts.

In the meantime, back at the Colne Valley Karate Club, life was in many ways typical of that era. The club comprised about twenty mixed grade members and was run by my first Karate instructor, John Baxter, a real Karate enthusiast who was a firm believer in the value of Basic Karate. The club was affiliated to Walter Seaton's England Karate Wado Kai (EKW) and met twice a week for either two hours of Kata practice or a gruelling and often laborious two hours worth of basic Junzuki (stepping front punch) or basic Gyakuzuki (stepping reverse punch). The combinations rarely exceeded three techniques and the intermittent sets of push ups, sit ups, squat and the odd barefoot run usually ensured that the majority of newcomers never stayed the course. As my interest increased, I remember purchasing the odd martial arts publication, and began to be inspired by stories about fighters such as Tyrone White.

Hand conditioning at the Huddersfield Karate Club during the late 70's.
"Fighting John Wright", pictured on the left, steadying the blocks

After watching "Enter the Dragon" at the cinema I was well and truly bitten by the martial arts bug.

In December 1978 I joined the Huddersfield Karate Club (also affiliated to the EKW), a town centre club founded by the highly respected Dave Allen. Its membership was massive, a class of eighty adult Karate Kas was the norm, out of which stood out about six Dan grades. Prior to joining the Huddersfield club, I'd never actually seen a real black belt instructor since, back then (especially in the North of England) black belts were fairly few and far between. Colne Valley's John Baxter was a first kyu brown belt, but to watch him perform Chinto Kata you'd think him a grand master. You see then, there was undoubtedly a massive difference between what was expected of a brown belt and what is evidently expected of a brown belt today.

Nowadays, students often expect to pass their belts just for turning out to the grading. It's hardly surprising that many of the hardcore clubs have already begun to phase out the use of belts and gradings, a system designed to encourage good all round martial arts development. In the late seventies and early eighties it was a very different story. You'd seldom see anyone wearing a black belt, or for that matter a brown belt grade, unless they were worthy to do so. Between 1979 and 1981 by own class attendance increased to between six and seven classes a week, and by 1980 I managed to grade to the respected brown belt.

Back then; the Huddersfield Karate Club had a very tough reputation.

This was due to its unique line up of seasoned combatants. One guy I remember used to run miles bare foot to class and then back home after class - his training sessions became legendary.

Another was the awesome looking Neil Habergam, a sort of throwback from the Phil Milner days. Mr Habergam spoke his mind and was always straight to the point both on and off the mats. He was banned from many competitions since he often sent his opponents unconscious to the nearest hospital. Neil used to turn up on the odd Thursday evening because Thursday was usually sparring night. Other names such as Julian 'Rubber Legs' Wiley, Neil Kane, Donnie Wray, Phil Robinson (who looked a bit like Freddie Mercury) and Nieman Sahota Singh have stuck with me.

I'm sure these names mean almost nothing to you, however they all played an important role in my own martial arts development. One man stood out head and shoulders above the rest: John Wright, or should I say 'fighting' John Wright for those who knew him well. John was fast, sharp, had a good tournament record and, by the time I arrived on the scene, had begun to carry a little weight around his midsection (John liked his beer). However, most people feared him because he never entertained idiots and seldom suffered fools gladly. In retrospect, John had a bit of a short fuse and, like most true warriors; he felt fear but never let it show.

In pursuit of the perfect side kick.
Bob Sykes and Paul Omalley, Bridlington course EKW 1980

Those hard, hard sparring sessions.

I recall one incident when a 6ft 7in French speaking Karate Ka visited out club and literally laid waste to many of the Dan grades during a typical Thursday evening sparring session. It was likely that Sensei Wright felt the pressure as this chap was massive and hell, could he kick. Everyone, including myself, who'd just come to the end of receiving my weekly beating off Phil (Freddie Mercury) Robinson, stopped when John Wright shouted across the training hall, 'Come on then lad, let's have a go then'. You could have cut the atmosphere with a knife. My mouth went dry and I felt the hairs on the back of my neck stand up. I had butterflies in my stomach and I wasn't even fighting this seemingly indestructible Frenchman. With a slight nod, but at the same time maintaining eye contact, the Frenchman accepted the challenge and quickly led off with two powerful lead leg roundhouse kicks, the second of which Sensei Wright stepped away from at a forty-five degree angle and swept the Frenchman's supporting leg. As those who ever sparred John Wright will know, he could sweep a person's leg away as well as any Judoka and this particular incident was no exception,

such was the conviction of the technique. As the Frenchman landed spread-eagled on his back, he felt the full wrath of John who, in true balletic fashion, leapt the full length of the fallen titan, landing with his heel to the head. I was gob smacked. The entire incident had, on the face of it, unravelled in slow motion. The composure, timing and brilliance of this manoeuvre had to simply be seen to be believed.

In a matter of seconds, Fighting John Wright had dismantled and destroyed a giant of a man, who had moments earlier appeared indestructible. I was totally inspired by a Sensei, who in many ways, became my mentor and would later become my forge.

Our author pictured with the "French Cat", Dominique Valera.

The Huddersfield WADO outward bound team, 1981.

Significant dates regarding British karate

1957. The first pictures of karate kas training in Britain are published in the Romford recorder.

1957. The first film (in black & white) of karate in Great Britain is taken by independent television.

1959. The first karate book published in Britain appears ' The manual of karate'

1962. Roy Stanhope begins training in karate.

1964. The British karate association is formed.
(Still in operation the BKA is the UK's oldest karate association.)

1965. Ticky Donovan the UK's Number one karate coach begins training under Tatsu Suzuki.

1965. The first British karate championships are held.

1968. Walter Seaton is awarded his black belt in Shotokan. Walter later became chief instructor of the EKW. (England karate WADO KAI) he was to later become a major influence on karate in the north east.

1971. Phil Milner- Yorkshires karate hard man ran from John O'Grants to Lands End in bare feet. Yorkshire television covered the story when Milner's karate club demolished an old church. They flattened it in just over five hours, with their bare hands and feet.

1972. Fighting Arts magazine is published by Terry O'Neil.

1976. The British karate team wins world championships. Ticky Donovan, Terry O'Neil, Stan Knighten and Billy Higgins were among the team members.

1983. Roy Stanhope of Manchester forms U K A S K O
(United Kingdom All-styles Karate Organisation)

1986. Great Britain wins the 8th world karate championships.

1989. World karate champion Vic Charles receives MBE.

1990. Great Britain Win the world karate championships for the fifth time in succession.

2000. Phil Milner dies.

The Awesome Terry O Neil ~ A legendary figure to emerge from those early Karate years.

Chinto KATA

Bob Sykes demonstrates his own version of Chinto KATA. Although synonymous with many KARATE systems Chinto's real roots reside in Chinese styles such as the snake and crane, both of which are still to this day evident within many of the KATA's moves. However my finished Chinto is nowadays more influenced by the southeast Asian systems, still I hope you can appreciate some of the similarities.

1. Attention   *2. Respect*   *3. Ready*

7. Punch   *8. Salute block*   *9. Cover*

4. *Close*   5. *Evade, cover or grab*   6. *Strike*

10. *Turn and strike hammer fist*   11. *Pull back*   12. *Strangle*

13. **Knee**   14. **Jump kick**   15. **Strangle**

19. **Step through and throw**   20. **Attack - SHOUT!**   21. **Twist and strike**

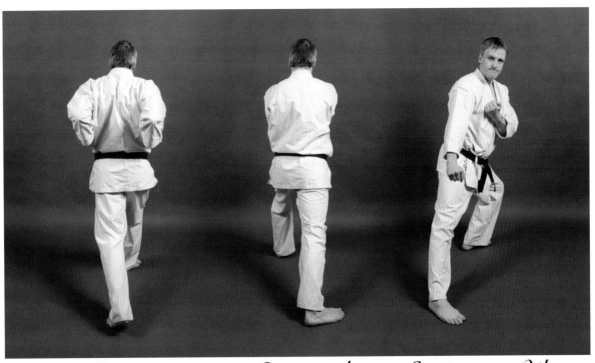

16. *Turn*   17. *Step strangle*   18. *Create space and throw*

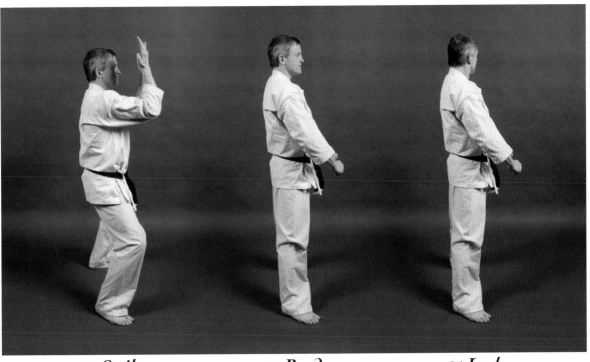

22. *Strike*   23. *Ready*   24. *Look*

25. **Break and strike**   26. **Twist**   27. **Break and strike**

31. **Break**   32. **Ready**   33. **Prepare**

28. Twist   *29. Break and strike*   *30. Drop weight and strangle*

34. Twist   *35. Twist*   *36. Close*

37. Open   *38. Prepare*   *39. Kick*

43. Prepare   *44. Kick*   *45. Reverse punch*

40. Punch   *41. Close*   *42. Open*

46. Open   *47. Prepare*   *48. Kick*

49. *Reverse punch*   50. *Twist back hand strike*   51. *Elbow*

55. *180°*   56. *Prepare*   57. *Kick*

52. *Pull back*   53. *Strike*   54. *Spin*

58. *Step and punch*   59. *Escape (twist)*   60. *Finish / Smile*

The *Karate Years* Part 2

It's quite possibly an indication of my age but ask me to recount what I was doing last month and I'd probably hesitate in my reply. However, the vivid imagery and often recited chronicles regarding my early competitive years seem, somehow, to be a far easier subject to recollect.

The time in question was August 1980 and the place was the 5-a-side indoor football pitch of the familiar Huddersfield Sports Centre. I found myself amongst the elite brown and black belts of the then renowned Huddersfield Wado Ryu Karate Club. It was a sort of pre-session meeting for an up and coming martial arts event which was to be held somewhere in Bradford. Back then I was always a fool for volunteering, seminars and tournament outings were no exception. Looking back, there was always a nervous edge to the gatherings. I don't really know why as half of those who put their names down to fight didn't turn out anyway. As I received my fearful nod of acceptance from Phil Robinson the team captain and coach, a gesture that indicated I was in the squad, I remember thinking: What's the worst thing that could possibly happen?

Although at the time we were not solely a competition orientated club, free sparring often took precedence over other activities such as Kata and the (then popular) set sparring scenarios such as Sanbon and Ohyo Gumite. This was mainly due to the enthusiasm of instructor Phill Robinson, who very much enjoyed and further encouraged a freestyle element in many of his classes.

Mr Robinson's Sunday morning gatherings in the Huddersfield Sports Centre combat room were often the best sessions of the week with lots of fitness, lots of conditioning and loads of free sparring.

Much of this was influenced by the fact we'd often travel down to take part in the very successful Dominique Valera seminars, hosted by Ishin Ryu's very own Ticky Donovan. Seminars such as these were revolutionary at the time. To watch the "French Cat", Dominique Valera, repeatedly kick his sparring partners at will, appeared in many ways unreal. I'd often look on in amazement as Mr Valera sparred all comers, occasionally chambering his knee and fend off up to five black belt opponents at one time, whilst hopping forwards.

In truth, Dominique Valera was a real showman, who possessed a rare and unique fighting style that, to this day, I've never seen anyone able to replicate.

Pictured in action: Kicking is Dominique Valera.

(Photo compliments of the Huddersfield Examiner).

The Huddersfield Karate Club 1981: Kneeling is coach Phil Robinson. Some pictured are no longer with us whereas others still train to this day. By the way the weird looking kid stood dead centre wrote this book.

In my mind, it was seminars such as these that were instrumental in bringing sport martial arts to life. In many ways it introduced us all to a new era. Ticky's training methods and input had, for me, made sparring more fun and effective and by the end of 1980 I'd been well and truly introduced to stripy Karate trousers and kick boots. Initially, however, this newer southern approach did not go down too well with many of the North Eastern Karate establishments. I recall entering an event in Sunderland where I was outright disqualified simply for stepping out onto the competition area wearing a pair of red kick boots.

I didn't even receive a refund on my entry fee. Having said that, back in those days entry fees posed no real problem, it was travelling those vast distances that bothered me most. This left me wondering why I was journeying up and down the country to look inside yet another red brick sports centre hall, often adding insult to injury by getting myself annihilated in the early elimination rounds. In any case, Bradford was near on local and then promoter Dave Brown had a more innovative approach to his events, mixing and matching Kung Fu and Karate exponents and introducing the occasional Kickboxing bout.

1981 Sparring Dominique Valera under the watchful eye of Ticky Donovan
Inset: Our author training outdoor's during the 1980's

All this, and the promised appearance of the legendary Steve Babbs, certainly made attending this event an attractive option. My memory of the event is patchy at best, however I do recall spending most of the day at mat side, viewing contest after contest it was nothing really to write home about. Every now and then the tournament would stop to allow for the odd Kung Fu or abstract Ninjitsu demonstration, some of which went on for so long that I'd forget what I was doing there in the first place. Suddenly, my name was called out over the tannoy, 'R. Sykes', Red, followed by my opponent, 'Owen Murry, White'. It seemed that the promoter was on first name terms with my rival.

My mind rushed back to the day before when I'd read a magazine article entitled "Murry's Magic", detailing how this hardened competitor, despite only having one had, was fast making a name for himself on Britain's open tournament circuits.

There was I in the summer of 1980, very much naive and underweight eighteen year old, facing a larger than life Karate legend. In truth I was early elimination cannon fodder and, to this day, flashbacks still persist of Mr Murry charging forward, sweeping both of my legs and, as I landed, hitting me with his padded yet hardened stump.

In retrospect the whole event became a bit of a learning curve, none of us reached so much as the quarterfinals and we all left early, not getting to see Steve Babbs in action.

Then, to top it all off, just a few days later I had to have my dog put down for attacking the next-door neighbour!

However, Huddersfield Karate Club did see better days and we'd regularly pick up more than our fair share of trophies at "The Quest for Champions" held in Belle Vue, Manchester. The Quest was usually held about twice a year and was hosted by the late Danny Connor of the British Karate Association. Danny ran the BKA from his Oriental World shop on Swan Street, Manchester. The Oriental World was a magical place; often it was a hive of activity. Especially on Saturday mornings, when sometimes you could meet up and speak with kick boxers of the likes of Brian Seabright and Lance Lewis. Over the years I've got to know both Brian and Lance quite well. Both now train at the Colne Valley Black Belt Academy near Huddersfield, where Lance in particular has had a huge influence on the way I now move and view the martial arts. Back in 1980, Lance Lewis was a kickboxing phenomenon and it's reassuring to know that, years on, the martial arts still play a vital role in his life as it so evidently does with many others of that unforgotten era.

Me and my first trophy - Quest for Champions, Champion 1981.

Techniques of Karate

Learn with Salvatoré Greenwood 3rd Dan, Bob Sykes 6th Dan. Master Bernard Taylor 5th Dan and Simon Jasper 3rd Dan.

Fig. 1.1 **Fighters square off**

Fig. 1.2 **Master Bernard Taylor punches, Simon Jasper blocks**

Fig. 1.4 **Note it's very important to both pull back and twist the withdrawn arm. This is where one first discovers the Ju Jitsu element of Karate Do**

Fig. 1.3 ***Then pulls opponent off balance with retracting hand and simultaneosly punches down at a 45° angle***

Fig. 2.1 **Fighters ready**

Fig. 2.2 **Simon throws a leadhand jab, Master Taylor switches levels with the use of a deep horse riding stance and delivers a front punch to the ribs**

Fig. 3.1 **Fighters ready**

Fig. 3.2 **Attacker moves in behind a solid reverse punch and Bob Sykes strikes the incoming arm**

Fig. 3.3 **Then moves off at a 45° angle to redefine center line (still maintaining control over his opponent's balance). Our author prepares a...**

Fig. 3.4 *Forearm strike to the neck*

Fig. 3.5 *And finishes with a well placed knee strike*

Fig. 4.1 **Fighters ready**

Fig. 4.2 *Master Taylor unleashes a close jab,*
Mr Greenwood blocks and strikes

Fig. 4.3 *Pulls, covers and...*

Fig. 4.4 *Locks up his opponent*

Fig. 5.1 **Fighters ready**

Fig. 5.2 **Sykes throws a superb lead leg roundhouse kick one of which Mr Greenwood blocks**

Fig. 5.3 *Mr Greenwood then launches a counter attack by preparing to kick*

Fig. 5.4 *Bob steps off the inside of the kick and strikes the inside knee with a familiar Karate Gedan technique*

Fig. 5.5 **Grabs and punches**

Fig. 5.6 and Fig. 5.7 **steps in...**

Fig. 5.8 Sweeps...

Fig. 5.9 And...

Fig. 5.10, Fig. 5.11 and Fig. 5.12 Steps over for a fashionable finish

The *Freestyle Years*

Remember, remember the fifth of November? I can, more especially that of 1984. It was around 8.30pm on a Monday when I found myself just yards outside the Caribbean Centre, Toxteth, Liverpool. I shall never forget the pain as, like a snake, I reeled on the ground, fighting for my breath, fighting for my life. All things considered, this was another fine mess I'd landed myself in.

*S*uddenly my body began to straighten out as it received an overdue intake of oxygen. I clambered to my feet and looked up in time to see a spectacular series of fireworks light up the night sky. Someone up there was looking out for me and that person wasn't Guy Fawkes.

I was living in the freestyle age, when coloured gis were all the rage. Those who took part in Britain's Open Tournament circuits during this time will certainly remember what exciting times they were. The old had finally given way to the new. The seeds sown by the early WACO fighters (the likes of Howard Brown and big Norman McKenzie, the respected Birmingham Lau and not forgetting the late Danny Connor), meant that open tournaments were numerous and competitors the length and breadth of Britain swarmed to them in droves. Some small groups began pulling away from the larger associations and taking control of their own licensing. Many others even began developing their own systems. In retrospect it wasn't so much a case of Do It Yourself Ryu, more an adaptation to a new way. For many of us at the time, the traditional stuff was just beginning to wear a bit thin. So with more pad work, fitness training and sparring, plus the abolition of Kata (unless performed to music) within many groups, the freestyle ethic was born.

Back in the early 80s, the British martial arts scene was very much a working class affair. Many of England's leading Karate Kas were born and bred in London's East End and in the Northeast of England in towns such as Stockton, Hartlepool and Newcastle the practise of martial arts was rife.

It appeared that anywhere that local industry was on the decline then martial arts were on the up. These were the good old days, before the release of 'Karate Kid', a time were you could actually give your sparring partner a good dig and they could hit you back without the fear of being sued.

At matside with the Liverpool Freestyle FSK's 1985

He didn't receive so much as a waza-ari (half point) for his efforts. Thankfully this never seemed to faze him, looking back it actually made him stronger in that occasionally he'd be forced to annihilate his opponent in order to win the bout. At a time when it appeared as though the entire martial arts establishment was against him, this freethinking freedom fighter positioned himself right at the cutting edge of the Freestyle movement.

It was during this period that Alfie Lewis, Liverpool Freestyle (previously Liverpool Lau), began to make a huge impact on Britain's Open Tournament circuit by proving supreme not only within the relatively new semi-contact events, but also within the much older regimented formats more suited to the men in white – some of whom were more than willing to compromise their dress code in order to entice Mr Lewis to take part in their events. There were those who appreciated Alfie's skill and genuinely wished him well, other however, were sadly more contemptuous towards him.

They viewed him as a threat and did all in their power to ensure that he wouldn't take the silverware back to Toxteth.

At times it both enraged and embarrassed me to witness the prejudice and biased decisions Alfie was forced to endure whilst carving out his reputation.

I watched on one occasion as he jumped high into the air, spun, and landed a well-controlled axe kick to the base of his opponent's skull.

But what was Freestyle? Well, it wasn't really a system, although during this period Alfie did collate a syllabus of his own, with principles taken from Karate, Kung Fu, Boxing and Judo. However the underlying message was that practitioners must mark any given method with a unique style of their own. In other words 'Don't be a look-alike and emulate somebody that you didn't know!' It was nothing new, at the time a lot of people were saying the same thing, it's just that too few were following their ideas through. These days I find it very amusing when systems proclaim themselves as being the 'ultimate' or the 'only' way, especially when they've never been tried or tested. Back on the semi-contact circuits of the early 80s there was none of that sort of nonsense because the truth was evident at each and every event. 'Thank you' would be the response of Kevin 'The Jedi' Brewerton each time his unstoppable blitzing technique was acknowledged.

Living in the Freestyle age - 1985 The Caribbean Centre in Taxteth, Liverpool. Our author is pictured far right standing
Others include Steve French, Charlton Abbey, Andrew Boyce, Peter (Overdog) Opara, Wayne Alcock and Alfie Lewis

The Taekwondo Association of Great Britain (TAGB), led by a relatively young Dave Oliver, would boldly go where no Taekwondo association had gone before, of for that matter since, when Dave unleashed Taekwondo's cream of the crop onto the semi-contact circuit. The result saw the likes of Kenny Walton, Kim Stones, Toney Sewell and Nigel Banks become respected all rounders. Having said that, no one messed with the Lau, they'd been a domineering force since the days of Steve Babbs and Frankie Lynce during the mid to late 70s. Old school fighters such as Neville Wray, Alvin Mighty, Mark Aston, Humphrey Broomes and Clive Parkinson were just the tip of the iceberg. As the late Danny Connor would remark, 'it's where the energy was', meaning anyone who was worth their salt, ventured out and became part of this incredible scene.

The theory was to design a competitive structure for many of the mainstream systems; Taekwondo, Kung Fu and Karate etc, to compete in and develop a martial arts melting pot. But add in a team of desperados from Toxteth and what evolved could be more closely likened to a ferocious meat grinder. Many bouts were fast and furious as opposing systems clashed head on. Liverpool Freestyle, at the time a club squad with many of its fighters living within a mile of the Caribbean Centre, Toxteth, was out beating national squads.

Perhaps Liverpool Freestyle had a secret formula? By this time, my own training regime had adjusted itself to suit the age. It consisted of lots of roadwork (a little too much at times), stacks of stretching (I could do the splits, honest!) plus most days, along with my brother Tony, working on impact kicking and combination kicking.

We'd leave the evening open to do as much free sparring as we could possibly fit in. By the time I arrived in Liverpool in October 84 I was more than prepared for whatever the freestyle boys had to throw at me.

The atmosphere on those Monday evenings was electric, as the Caribbean Centre, Toxteth revealed to me its hidden code: 'hard training', 'hard training' and more 'hard training'.

They say that success breeds success and I noticed my own level raise within a matter of weeks. A few months prior to joining the Liverpool Freestyle club Id had the honour of facing Mr Lewis at the Yorkshire Open, held on the 4th July in Bradford. It was during the team semi finals and I couldn't believe my luck as, after much deliberation with Manchester's Simon Howe who captained our team, I was allowed to step out as number one fighter for the squad. To me it was the fight of a lifetime. To Alfie Lewis it was just another semi final en route to a championship win. He probably figured he'd do just enough to win since, on the face of it, I wasn't really the most intimidating of characters. To cut a short story even shorter, after much in the way of overenthusiastic kicking, I managed to catch Alfie with a lucky jumping spinning back kick.

The kick in question - when Bob met Alfie
The Yorkshire Open July 4th 1984

Although winded by the kick, he was still somehow able to deliver a well-timed reverse punch to my back, for which he received, IPPON!

It wasn't at the time uncommon for the reverse punch to override just about every other technique, especially at Karate events such as the Yorkshire Open. With the 'ippon' giving Alfie the bout, I left the are body intact and Alfie took his revenge in the finals by knocking his much larger Karate opponent clean out with the fastest jumping spinning kick I'd ever seen.

Although Alfie had long since let the whole incident go, it had in fact gone right to my head and I just couldn't stop going on about it. 'Blah blah blah, when I hit Alfie with a back kick, blah.'

The whole thing came to a head at the Caribbean Centre on the 5th November 1984. Everyone partnered up to spar, as always I headed for Alfie and this time I was up for it! And he'd most probably had just about enough of me.

Perhaps it's just me going off on one again but it was as though that particular evening, something else was at play. I can't put my finger on it, even to this day, but everything seemed so clear, so clean and in many ways heightened as Alfie hit me with a sidekick which knocked me the lengthen of the centre. I was stubbornly quick to regain my footing and launch myself back, to be greeted by the best back kick I'd ever had the displeasure to receive – I thought it had split my spleen as my bent body quickly hit the deck. After about thirty seconds there had been zero change in my condition.

I remember a few guys kicked open the emergency fire doors and got me outside, at first I thought they were throwing me out to finish me off.

The distance just wasn't quite right for my jumping spinning kick
Yorkshire Open Alfie v Bob 1984

A roundhouse kick falls short
Yorkshire Open team semi finals July 4th, 1984

All joking aside, the lesson had been well learned. As I walked back through the fire doors with my head held low, Andrew Boyce enquired 'Are you OK Bob?' to which I replied 'Yeah'.

Alfie looked relaxed and when I asked him to continue sparring he just looked at me, laughed and said 'I think we've done enough Bob'. A statement from which I somehow managed to draw a morsel of dignity.

So, remember, remember the fifth of November
Gunpowder, treason and plot
For I see no reason why the freestyle season
Should ever be forgot

Alfie Lewis / Bob Sykes 2006

Competitors of the Age.

Liverpool's, Peter O Para was a star fighter to emerge from the early freestylescene.

Humphry Brooms became a household name in both semi contact & full contact events

Bob Fermor became a respected master of the freestyle form.

Techniques of Freestyle

Learn with Alfie Lewis, numerous World Titles and tipped by many to be Britain's best tournament fighter to date.

Fig. 1.1 ***Robbie Hughes moves in behind lead leg side kick***

Fig. 1.2 ***Alfie cuts the angle***

Fig. 1.3 **Then delivers a well placed back fist**

Fig. 2.1 **Fighters ready**

Fig. 2.2 **Robbie chambers to kick**

Fig. 2.3
Alfie changes
the line...

*Fig. 2.4 **And connects with a powerful groin kick***

*Fig. 3.1 **Fighters square off***

*Fig. 3.2 **Alfie sweeps his opponents lead leg***

Fig. 3.3 **And then...**

Fig. 3.4 **Finishes Robbie off with a ridge hand strike**

The **Kickboxing Years**

Permit me to let you in on a little secret. During my teens I was inspired and motivated by Benny 'The Jet' Urquidez, so much so that at times I wanted to be just like him. Over twenty years on, my good friend, training partner and personal Guru, Lance Lewis likens my character more to that of the late Danny Connor. Not what I originally envisioned. However, at the tender age of forty-four, this newer image suits me quite well. In fact, I feel rather privileged for Lance to view me in this manner.

*A*t the end of the day, Danny was a great originator and played an essential part in Lance's development in becoming Britain's most respected kick boxer. I'd prefer to view myself as being a sort of cross between Connor and Urquidez, although I'd be ill matched against Danny's vocabulary and razor sharp wit and my kickboxing career in o way resembled that of Benny 'The Jet'. In hindsight, I was probably more of a Bobby 'The Bet' as you could usually bet your bottom dollar that I wasn't going to win. Nevertheless, it was fun while it lasted and, not unlike many fighters of the period, I've a few stories to tell.

Let's back track in time to October 1986. The venue was Victoria Leisure Centre, Nottingham, where I found myself topping the bill, fighting against Kash 'The Flash' Gill, for the then vacant

A rare win for 'Bobby the Bet'

British PKA light middleweight title – during a time when full contact kickboxing and Thai boxing were on the up and up. Reputable opponents were numerous and kickboxing events were being staged just about everywhere.

In Manchester, Oldham and much of the Northeast, Thai boxing undoubtedly ruled, with Thai greats such as Master Toddy, Master Woody and Master Sken who between them produced a good few world-class competitors.

Birmingham and the West midlands were home to the Professional Karate Association (PKA). Proper full contact – eight kicks above the waist and all that. Yes, Birmingham was Hawk's roost where World Kickboxing champion Howard Brown headed a stable of kick boxers, champions all, the likes of Steve Miknenas, Kash 'The Flash' Gill and the very respected Lawrence White. Down in London it seemed as though everybody was at it. Phil Mayo's Contact Kickboxing Association (CKO) was growing larger by the day and newer London promoters such as Alan Mortlock were beginning to make an impression.

Training days Dave Barry, Lance Lewis, Richard Sykes and yours truly

Did you know that these days author Pat O'Keefe fought the famous boxer Nigel Benn at kick boxing at Alan Mortlock's first show? It was a three round contest that Benn won in the third round. They were strange days and there's little doubt that the aforementioned fighters were on top of their game.

In my own division I had the privilege to fight against the likes of Gary Osbourne. Some readers may remember the Bloxwich Boxer who eventually became a master kicker. I often wonder what happened to Gary Osbourne who I remember giving me one hell of a pasting in London back in 1985. Having said that, back in those days it was often me who did most of the kicking. A factor which resulted in me being ranked above fighters who I'd previously lost out

to; hard hitters such as Derek Iddon of Preston. Derek was a short, stocky fighter with a powerful right hand, which he delivered sometimes in the form of a cross and on occasions in the form of a sort of hook. Yes, Derek did lose from time to time but more often than not, his hard right hand was certain to spell doom for his opponents. Derek stopped me during the fourth round at a CKO show held in Warrington. No lie, my head hurt for a week but it didn't matter one bit; I was simply hooked on kickboxing. So much so that in 1985, during a one-week period, I fought in three separate kick boxing shows. In March of 1986 I fought in two different shows both on the same day. During this era, London's Chris McNeash kicked me, Birmingham's Derek Edwards punched me and Jeff Bullock of Ormskirk literally tried to kill me during a bout in Warrington.

Nigel Benn in action on Alan Mortlock's first show
Picture courtesy of Martial Arts Illustrated and Alan Martlock

At the time, Jeff seemed to be at his peak, he was undoubtedly a hard-hitting fighter with a reputation to match. For years I'd followed Jeff's rise to fame through reading reports in the martial arts press. I recall one story regarding Jeff that reported his match with the renowned northern Muay Thai fighter Junior Salmon who suffered a dislocated shoulder when Jeff dispatched him from the ring with the use of a then unorthodox Ju Jitsu throw.

After this many realised that the clinch was a definite no go area for anyone who wanted to go the distance with this Ormskirk hard man.

Throughout our particular encounter, Mr Bullock was once again unwilling to

A victory over British Champion, Colin Barret during the 1985 World Championship

comply with the rules. I recall that each time we clinched he wrapped his leg round mine and dropped his weight to the floor in an attempt to do damage to my leg. It seemed an almost suicidal tactic for me to get drawn into the clinch again, so with the use of a mobile stance, cat like reflexes and a lightning fast jab, I was able to keep my distance, and more importantly, go the distance, with a far more formidable and experienced fighter than myself. A draw for me was a good result and along with the fact that just prior to this bout I'd received a victory over British CKO champion Colin Barrett during the WAKO World Championships was an indication that things were finally looking up for yours truly.

Sykes Jab's - Barret

Jumping back kick

Bob Sykes and Arther O'Louglin share a victory

There I was back in 1986, facing Kash 'The Flash' Gill, getting myself ready to start our seven round contest for the light middleweight crown. Kash, who was fresh back from his World Amateur Full Contact win in the sleepy Gallic town of St Nazire and who had prior to that, beaten Taekwondo's Kenny Walton in the Combat Karate TV pilot, was in a serious mood. 'Pain for Bob Sykes' was his prediction. This I felt could have been due to our first meeting (in the same year) in Sheffield, during which I'd taken him the full distance, where although Kash received a win to his credit, it hadn't necessarily been a clear-cut decision.

I don't know about you but referee Arther O'Louglin looks more worried than Bob

kickboxing crazed southpaw.

Anyway, I'd an ally in the ring, as refereeing was none other than Arthur of the Britons, aka Arthur O'Loughlin. Arthur was a good friend and certainly the best kick boxer ever to emerge from Yorkshire. What made him my ally? Well I think that you can work that one out for yourselves.

Our author redefines centerline and drives in with his trade mark- the spinning back kick

In any case, there I was, stood face to face with a fellow kick boxer who was intent on doing me some serious damage.

I recall not being all that bothered by the whole occasion, I was more fascinated by the fact that over one thousand spectators had come to watch. Further more, contrary to common belief, I did feel more than capable of beating this six foot one,

Kash 'The Flash' leg kicks our author in the 2nd round!

On the ropes with Kash 'The Flash' Gill

Now please excuse my boasting but during the first round I did fight out of my skin, throwing kick upon kick – jumping back kick, spinning kick, roundhouse. I remember an instant in which time momentarily froze; it was when my right roundhouse kick connected with the left side of Kash Gill's head. However, no matter how many kicks I threw, I still felt I was losing out to Kash's right jab (I can still to this day feel it bouncing off my forehead). Round two continued at the same hectic pace with my sporadic kicking outbursts being met by the Flash's back leg round kick and flurries of overhand and hooking punches.

Real aliveness. This is about when things went a bit 'pear shaped' in the 3rd round

Things were beginning to look grim and, as Bey Logan put it at the time, 'the writing was on the wall'.

Now this may seem a little too abstract foe some readers, but during a crucial part of our contest my entire perception of time began to slow down. It was when, as it was reported in Britain's leading martial arts publication at the time, I connected with a booming right cross to the top of Gill's head. It was also assumed that if this punch had landed a little lower the outcome might have been different. Yes, as the punch hit its mark, everything slid into a state of slow motion and what noise there was seemed irrelevant. What must have been only two or three seconds seemed somehow to stretch itself out into ten or twelve seconds. It's nothing new, many athletes have had almost identical peak performance experiences, and they call it 'being in the zone'. Those of you reading who have been there will know what I'm talking about, those who haven't – there's still something for you to look forward to. Having admitted that my peak performance wasn't enough to match the skill and determination of Kash 'The Flash' Gill who, after knocking me down three times in the third, proved to be the more superior athlete and twenty years on still dominates his weight division.

Our author takes a rest while the judges form their conclusions on the bout

Nowadays Kash and myself are good friends, furthermore I feel honoured to have shared the ring with him. His past is partly my past and my past is partly his. It was a golden age of kickboxing – a special era in which the events were full of character, the spectators were numerous and the fighters had magic in their eyes.

European Kickboxing Champion ~ Jeff Bullock.

Early 70's Kickboxing action.

Significant dates regarding the early spread of full contact and kickboxing within the UK.

1975. The first British full contact championships held in Belle-vue Manchester. The champions who emerged were Jim Cooper & Dave Cooper (Cornwall) Tony Burrows (Plymouth) Steve Babbs (Birmingham) Frankie Lynce (London)

1976. Howard Hanson Vs Arnold Urquidez was screened on, the world of sport ITV channel.

1977. Kickboxing shows are held in Manchester, London, and Birmingham etc. Fighters such as Lance Lewis, Steve Babbs, Godfrey Butler, Steve Taberner fly the flag for British full contact and kickboxing.

1978. Sporadic shows are held throughout the UK; hence kickboxing became a familiar feature within the martial arts scene.

1979. Lance Lewis KO's Howard Brown in defence of his British super-lightweight title.

Techniques of Kickboxing

Learn with four times world Kickboxing Champion, Kash 'The Flash' Gill.

Fig. 1.1 **Fighters square off**

Fig. 1.2 **Attacker throws a 'Thai style' leg kick, Kash blocks**

Fig. 1.3 **Prepares**

Fig. 1.4 **And finishes his opponent off with a well placed punch to the jaw**

Fig. 2.1 **Fighters ready**

Fig. 2.2 **Bob attempts an advanced trapping technique**

Fig. 2.3 **Quickly realizing Bob's game plan, Kash 'The Flash' retaliates with a 'Thai style' elbow strike**

Fig. 2.4 **Then clinches**

Fig. 2.5 **Knees to finish**

The *Wing Chun Wars*

It was early December 1986 when I found myself climbing up that windswept hill on the outskirts of Huddersfield. It could have been the steep climb but when I finally reached the top my knees were shaking and my mouth felt dry. After hacking my way through the undergrowth I was, to say the least, surprised to see the size of my reception committee. I remember feeling the hairs on the back of my neck stand up as I stepped out into the clearing to view the small fleet of sports cars, out of which stepped around 20 athletically built southerners, all of whom were wearing matching leather jackets and either jeans of tracksuit bottoms.

It was at the end of the day the 1980s and it was apparent that the tough guy look was to be the costume most favoured by the Derek Jones supporters club. It's a long story, but I'd somehow found myself smack bang in the middle of the Wing Chun wars. In the run up to this encounter the martial arts press of the day had somehow seemed fixated with events in Europe and the UK where martial arts teachers had been openly challenged and, in some cases, attacked and beaten by representatives from opposing groups. Thankfully much of the martial arts fraternity demonstrated a certain disapproval as they were subjected to press release after press release and, at times, actual film footage of these often thuggish looking affairs. I glanced to my left to see a small orange Citroën pull into the car park; I was surprised to see it had made it up the hill! Out clambered my brother Tony, soon to be Royal Marine Paul Belk, the new to the scene Pete 'the dumper truck' Brook and the old Huddersfield warhorse and former biker, Andy Dobson.

Only the day before I'd tried in vain to rally the troops, however a tournament in Barnsley had somehow taken priority where I'd fought with the then legendary kick boxer Arthur O'Loughlin. But that's another story. The Huddersfield four joined up with the solitary figure of Steve Blackburn, Steve was a hard hitting first Dan, the sort of guy you could always rely on in a crisis such as this. I remember spending a couple of moments trying to spot Master Derek Jones amongst the mass of heads, legs and black leather, all of which appeared to move towards the lone orange Citroën like a single oversized organism. 'Is your name Bob Sykes?' shouted a voice from within the pack. The question was aimed at my little brother Tony, who, at 6' 4" and over 16 stone of highly toned muscle stood out well amidst the Bob Sykes devotees.

What has since become a bit of an unreported phase in my life, was, for a short while after, much talked about and ridiculous stories began to circulate.

One tells of how Derek dispatched four of my best fighters with a combination of straight blast attacks and another where I was said to have knocked Derek out with a jumping spinning hook kick to the temple. Neither of these two resemble in any way the truth, however I do like the first best! The true (well my true) account is as follows:

'That's Bob Sykes over there'; Tony pointed his long and well-trained arm towards the clearing where I was standing in wait. For a split second time stood still as the visiting team all turned and simultaneously looked in my direction. What could I do? Run? For starters, my legs were frozen solid and the die had long been cast. The mass of black leather jackets began to move in my direction. I still hadn't been able to single Derek out. Then, all of a sudden, as if time itself had played some sort of evil trick on me, Derek was there right in front of me, hurling punch upon punch into my face. The paralysis lifted. This was actually happening! Still not having yet fully identified my foe, I felt to be grappling an extra large fitting leather jacket. After about 30 seconds of clinch work where heads clashed on more than one occasion, with the odd knee strike courtesy of Derek, surprise surprise, the fight fell to the ground. This was most probably my saving grace as neither Derek or myself had, at this point, trained groundwork. As we frantically rolled around, arm bars, leg locks or even 'ground and pound' were not the state of play. There was far too much biting and gouging to be considered. After what seemed to be an eternity on the wet grass, Derek somehow got to his feet first in order to continue his onslaught. Red mist perhaps, but the next thing I remember is standing up and throwing my jumper and T-shirt to the ground. My lungs felt as though they'd burst as I breathed in the cold December air. **'Come on then'**, I cried.

'Hit him Bob' shouted a recognisable voice from the hometown stand. We both began to move around as if to spar. 'Get him Derek' and 'Box him Bob' yelled the South and North, who had by this time formed a human enclosure for our conflict's final scene. I don't really care to romanticise the whole affair but for a few seconds I felt like Clint Eastwood in 'Every Which Way but Loose', one of his hit movies where he had played a bare-knuckle fighter.

Thud, thud, I unleashed two successive Thai style shin kicks, both of which met their mark. These were followed by a back kick, which, on impact, felt as though it had connected square on to a kicking shield (it must have been the leather jacket!) 'Use your hands, box him' bellowed big T.

It was possibly down to Derek's fingers finding my eyes whilst we'd pressure tested the wet ground or maybe that his 'Chip, Chung Chow' onslaught had fractured my cheekbone. Perhaps it was a combination of the two but all of a sudden spent as he was, Derek appeared to multiply into three identical yet hazy images. I opted for the middle one and let my cross go. The frozen skin and bone of my right hand connected well with the jaw of the warrior from Body, Mind and Spirit. Derek fell back onto one hand, there didn't look to be much more fight left in him. I remember seeing two Londoner's hands reach into their jackets. Maybe they were carrying? 'Get the guns out of the car', shouted a Huddersfield accent. There were no guns, but the bluff paid off as the South stepped a coupled of paces back.

There was no fight left in either Derek or myself, so I pulled him to his feet and proclaimed the fight a draw, which it was. I'd survived a close encounter with a real Wing Chun warrior – but only just. In hindsight I don't really know what drew Derek all the way from London up onto that desolate Northern hillside, courage perhaps? I can only really speak for myself, and the answer to that could well be open to question.

As for Derek and myself, we became great friends. Sadly he fell victim to a motorcycle crash a few years later.

After all that (and it's something Derek didn't know), it has come to my attention that, according to local history, the hill were we fought is said to be the hill referred to in the famous nursery rhyme ' Jack and Jill'. This is for Derek. God bless you, you were a true warrior.

Derek and Bob went up the hill
To see who was the Master
Bob fell down and broke his crown
And Derek came tumbling after.

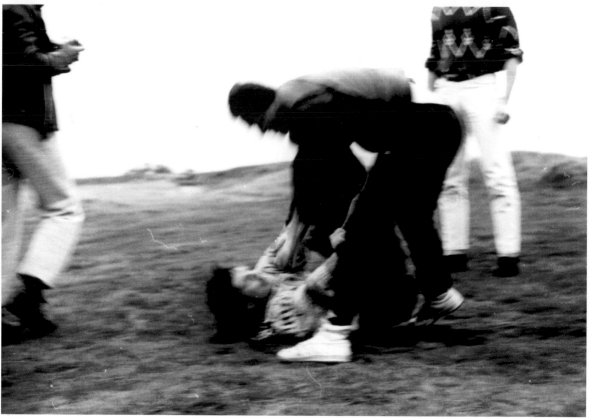

Kings of the Hill.
Derek Jones and Bob Sykes take time out for a post fight photo.

When Bob met Bill

It was late August when Bill 'Superfoot' Wallace returned to the UK to conduct a series of seminars, organised by Bill Judd of London. When I arrived at the Stretford Sports Centre, Manchester there already seemed quite a mixture of students amassing and awaiting the arrival of this larger than life legend. An unbeaten full contact champion and movie star, one who had for years been an inspiration, not only to myself but also to many around the world.

With a left leg that had been recorded as moving at over 60 miles per hour, Bill Wallace was and still is considered to be the cream of the crop when it comes to both Kickboxing and American Sport Karate. After a gruelling two-hour session that focussed on all aspects of kicking and following his unique demonstration on how to execute his famous kicking combos, the time arrived for free sparring.

I myself seized this opportunity to get in the first spar of the evening with the man himself. What many people present were unaware of was the fact that, a few months prior to this event, both Mr Wallace and myself had performed a demonstration bout for a cable TV network and furthermore, I was a little surprised that Bill actually remembered me from that day. At this point, people all around the country were beginning to familiarise themselves with my (then new) publication, Martial Arts Illustrated, which appeared to speak their language.

However, I was still first and foremost a martial artist and as such wanted to make a lasting impression. So, with an audience of about two hundred practitioners, amongst whom was literally everybody who was anybody in the Manchester martial arts community, plus one or two editors from the opposition and the then new martial arts media machine, Video Martial Arts (VMA). The stage was set as I set to work on Mr Wallace, who, incidentally, had similar ideas towards me. During our 15 minute spar, besides receiving a large swelling above my left eye and a few bruised ribs into the bargain, everyone present stopped to watch what was, for Bill and myself, nothing but an over zealous sparring session. However the wave of acceptance from the onlookers quickly eased my pain and the 'Well done Bob' from a martial arts legend such as Bill 'Superfoot' Wallace gave me such a boost that I'm still feeding off it to this day.

The author takes time out to examine the famous left leg of Bill "Superfoot" Wallace

The "Wallace" Jab

"It's mine Sykes" Wallace on the attack

A "Lucky" Back Kick finds it's mark

The *Warriors*

On the 4th March 2005, a few good friends met up and got together for the first time in years.

Many had travelled from different parts of the UK; all possessed contrasting skills and had for years trained in a diverse array of martial arts disciplines. However, they were all bound by one single denominator, they were all former members of a unique fighting squad, one that impacted the martial arts scene of the late eighties and the early nineties. That squad? The Warriors.

The Warriors were a group of fighters & competitors. Our supporters viewed us as larger than life martial arts personalities, our adversaries saw us as non-conformists or even troublemakers. However, I perceived us as a group of martial arts misfits desperate for a cause. One became fitting when Martial Arts Illustrated promoted its first martial arts spectacular, Clash of the Titans I. During the late eighties the entire martial arts scene was beginning to stagnate and become a little boring. I even remember falling asleep at a kickboxing show (the noise from the crowd couldn't keep me awake). So with Alfie Lewis acting as team coach, Joe Tierney as team captain and Peter O Para, Tony Sykes, Chris Williams, Jeff Bullock and Chris Boughey jumping on board, we formed The Warriors, a name

Our author blasts his way to yet another victory

given to us by the late Neil Williams. It was promotions such as Clash of the Titans that were responsible for giving us an outlet for a seemingly new energy, a force or vigour that on the face of it had the impetuous to change things, to rock the boat and, in many ways, upset the applecart.

Our author in flight against world Taekwondo champion Nigel Banks

In doing so we created our fair share of conflict and controversy.

Casting my mind back a few chapters to those ever so distant karate years, to the days when I'd hear amazing stories of the Birmingham Lau Gar squad. A squad that consisted of fighters with superhuman abilities such as Steve Babbs, Frankie Lynch, Neville Wray and other household names such as Clive Parkinson and Humphrey Broomes. This squad of Kung Fu guys dominated the seventies and the eighties when they beat in style all the leading karate kas and Korean stylists of the day. I'd always dreamed of being like those Lau guys and, come October 1990, well over two and a half thousand spectators had packed the stands at Granby Halls, Leicester to watch the British Lau Gar squad (the direct lineage of those aforementioned superhumans) take on the Warriors.

Earlier that evening, both teams had warmed up fighting the tough Korean Karate guys from the English Korean Karate Association (EKKA) in twenty bouts, many of which were not without contention.

Both teams were well aware of just what was at stake and it was by no means the one thousand pounds prize money. Joe Tierney of the Warriors took a decision over the talented Lau fighter Brian Nelson, then we lost a bout when Tom Wynne had his head split open by Scotland's Duncan Pollett.

The Warriors come out to play, Leicester 1990

Then yours truly messed up when I lost out to Gary Douglas on a split decision. Fighters lost and fighters won until everything hinged on the tenth and last bout.

'The Megatron', Nathan Lewis represented the honour of Lau Gar Kung Fu against my little brother Tony Sykes. It was sink or swim for Lau Gar who desperately needed a win to force a draw. It was reported that this bout gave off so much energy and electricity that the atmosphere within the stands and at mat side crackled. For those who were there, this was a bout of epic proportion and fifteen years on is still available from DVD from video stockists. To the disappointment and dismay of poor Nathan Lewis, Tony managed to take the bout with a unanimous decision. The rumble and the row of the then biggest crowd in martial arts rang out. The Warriors had, by beating the Great Britain Lau Gar squad,

achieved something special. Not bad for a kid who'd started Karate all those years ago at that low key Colne Valley Karate club. Not wanting to blow my own trumpet too much but, along with my much respected opponent Jackson White of the Taekwondo Association of Great Britain (TAGB), we were the first fighters to step out onto the mat at the first Clash of the Titans event. The rest, should I say, is martial arts history. Hence all the Warriors salute and pay tribute to all their hard-hitting opponents from those early events. Dave Oliver and his remarkable TAGB squad - we salute you. Neville Wray and the National Lau Gar squad - we salute you also. Last, but not least, Mick Blackwell and his hard-hitting EKKA - we salute you, for giving the Warriors some of their hardest bouts when we fought you on your home turf in Norwich back in 1991.

Victory over the Lau - The Warriors at Granby Halls, 1990

The Warriors today - From left to right - Tony Sykes, Chris Williams, Bob Sykes, Joe Tierney, Chris Boughey, John Dawson and Tom Wynne

Prior to the publication of this book I took time out to speak with my brother Tony to discover just what he thought of a team that fully exemplified a martial arts era.

Q: Who were the Warriors?

Tony: Basically, the Warriors were a group of fighters from different systems and different associations who formed over a gradual period of time to eventually develop into the team that is nowadays known famously as the Warriors.

Q: What memories spring to min regarding that first encounter with those high kicking Taekwondo chaps?

Tony: I've got lots of memories regarding that first Clash of the Titans event. Probably the most vivid of those recollections is of actually arriving at the venue. Having already attended many martial arts meetings and competitions over the years, the scale and energy from the spectators outside the venue was something not to dissimilar from what you'd expect to see outside a football stadium or pop concert. In a nutshell it certainly had something different about it!

Q: Looking back to the Clash of the Titans and beyond, do you feel surprised that you've in fact become one of the competitors most synonymous with that particular era?

Tony: Although I only competed in the first seven events (the early years), maybe it was

Tony Sykes Vs Richard Vince - Granby Halls

Jumping back kick connects - Sykes Vs Jackson white

the controversy, which surrounded many of my bouts. However I did feel that there were a lot of larger and more well established fighters such as Joe Tierney, certainly a little man with a big name, Peter O'Para, Chris Boughey and Chris Williams who really stood out with his unparalleled ability. Not forgetting the opposing teams who came along and took part. Squads which included competitors such as Richard Vince -the hard hitting Norfolk punch and the amazingly talented David Baptist of Lau Gar Kung Fu and Kim Stones and Kenny Walton who were legends within the TAGB. Just to be named alongside competitors of such high standing is to me an honour in itself.

Q: You mentioned controversy ~ why is it that people always appear to remember the controversial bouts?

Tony: That's an interesting point! Out of all the fights I took part in during those early Clash of the Titans years, I drew two, lost three and won four but like you say, people are more likely to focus on the more controversial bouts, which I can understand. Even today as I view a couple of those controversial bouts, in many ways they're not necessarily bouts that I am proud of, even though people often, still to this day, comment on them. Even leading martial artists who were not of that particular era and are quite famous in other martial arts endeavours are rather surprised and even a little excited at the footage. In retrospect it was just things that happened in the moment, often because the heavyweights of the team attracted so much in the way of attention that the pressure was often on the likes of Mark Osbourne (TAGB), Richard Vince (EKKA), Nathan Lewis (Lau Gar) and even myself.

Q: Back in 1990 at the Granby Halls, Leicester, the Warriors beat the British Lau Gar squad. Could you tell me your feelings regarding this incredible achievement?

Tony: I remember one instance around 18 months before the event, we were travelling back from winning the Cumbrian Open. You, Joe Tierney and Chris Williams were in the back of the car and Chris Williams remarked, "Just think, at this rate we will be beating the Lau Gar soon" and everybody just laughed at the idea.

At that time, the Warriors were just forming and lo and behold, not long after, we were at Granby Halls, holding our own and competing at that level.

Q: But to beat the Lau Gar when they had literally taken out just about every other team in the country from Karate to Taekwondo was, to say the least, a massive achievement?

Tony: The Lau Gar were obviously an awesome squad with an unmatched lineage. What's more, it was at a time when tournament Karate or tournament Kung Fu semi-contact fighting hit its peak

Q: What statement would you say sums up the Warriors squad?

Tony: A group of guys from different social backgrounds all of who became good friends.

Tony Sykes Vs Mark Osbourne - Clash of the Titans one

The Stick Years

In examining the stick fighting years, or should I say the fighting with a stick years, the hit movie The Matrix acts as a partial similarity. Those reading who are at all familiar with the film's story line may recall The Matrix as being representative of a false consciousness, when the system designed by mankind inadvertently turns the tables on its creator and mankind, oblivious to true existence, begin to serve the system rather than the system serving man.

It's a bit like the tail wagging the dog. Just how this relates to the stick fighting years should begin to unfold. For those still reading, it's back to October 1995. I was sitting comfortably at home contemplating the cosmos when I heard a 'tap tap tap' on my front door. I opened it to find one of my students (Nigel Brown) standing outside with two homemade Eskrima sticks. 'Did you get my stuff from London?' he enquired. My mind quickly raced back to the week before when I'd discussed the possibility of beginning training in the art of Eskrima. Nigel – who some readers may remember played 'Lumpy Brown' in an early Martial Arts Illustrated (MAI) comic series, 'Martial Mayhem', a sort of 'sheep in wolf's clothing' character – had previously attended a stick fighting seminar hosted by a local Tai Chi instructor, where he'd semi perfected the heaven six count double stick drill and been pestering me for months to contact any reputable UK based Eskrima groups. I pointed to the far corner of my living room where there sat two instructional video tapes and six spanking new rattan sticks, all sent up courtesy of John Harvey and Pat 'The Cat' O'Malley of Rapid Arnis International. Nigel responded with one of his distinctive superior smiles and the stick years began.

Those early years, which can be categorised as the blue stick years, were actually quite fun, as both Nigel and myself familiarised ourselves with the basic Eskrima vs. Eskrima motions; many, interesting as they were, often dropped into the realms of choreography. Having said that, it was a lot more enjoyable getting our heads round the basic flow drills such as Hubud, Box Pattern, Punio Sumbrada and the all too common Sinawali double stick drills, all of which where, for want of a better expression, superfluously necessary. At the time, many of the drills were being taught to both Nigel and myself by John Harvey and Pat O'Malley, whose help and guidance proved invaluable during those early Eskrima years. I remember attending a seminar held somewhere near Leeds with a famous Thai Boxing friend, Ronnie Green. It was during this seminar that I first met Jude 'The Clubber of Men' Tucker, whose all round understanding of stick fighting mechanics impressed both Ronnie and myself. It was as though he was operating on a different level and really put into context a lot of what I had previously been trying to understand about this seemingly complicated art form.

All for one and one for all - The WEKAF years, our author pictured with winning Eskrimadors Nigel Brown, Patrick O'Malley and the unmistakable John 'Papos' Harvey

In retrospect, those early years – complex as they may have seemed – were not without diversity as I often found myself studying up to three different systems at any one time. A bonus, I suppose, exclusive to martial arts editors who operate outside the political dogma that taints many small groups, especially those of the stick fighting realms. Leeds based Jonathon Aray helped me greatly in getting used to drills such as heaven six etc. Brian Jones of Peterborough introduced me to the very effective art of Latosa. Master Danny Guba and Master Percival Pableo influenced me greatly with their representation of the fast and furious art of Doce Pares and Dave Barry (Rebel Dog) initiated me into stick sparring with a difference. Crash helmets, heavy sticks and no holds barred style, it was definitely no place for the faint hearted, Although at the time I was having a lot of fun competing, fist by winning the Midland Area Championships and then during the same year, out pointing the then world silver medallist, Andy Gibney, I still felt I was existing in an artificial world and really needed to get to grips with a Filipino art that was indigenous to it country of origin.

It was during late '98 when Geoff Thompson (who needs little introduction to those readers who read MAI) put me in touch with MAI's now renowned cross training columnist, Rick Young.

Our author takes time to advise Dave Berry how to beat his foe

Rick had already begun writing the odd article for MAI and invited me to one of his Edinburgh seminars, where he hosted the Guro himself, Dan Inosanto. Prior to meeting Rick, I'd already had the pleasure of training with Jeet Kune Do's Phil Norman, who'd been active in putting the record straight when he attended a Black Eagle Day, a report of which appeared in MAI, and who, after visiting my good self, left me limping with a very badly bruised leg. Not put off by this, I made a pilgrimage to Edinburgh and was simply blown away by Guro Dan's skill, understanding and articulation of the art of Kali, JKD and Brazilian Ju Jitsu.

His knowledge was, to my mind, unparalleled as he demonstrated a whole host of contrasting Filipino arts, always careful to credit their origin and the instructors who had so trustingly passed their understanding into his modest and capable hands. Prior to this edification I'd begun to think of myself as some sort of stick fighting authority, however I was so humbled by Dan Inosanto's skill and dexterity that, for me, it was back to the drawing board. Not too long after attending the Edinburgh seminar I was contacted by Jose Bernado, who was of Filipino origin, who invited me to train in the art of Delastiko (the rubber band style).

Bob with Guru Dan Inosanto

Jose was a small, meek and very quiet master, whose only condition was no photos, no publicity, just training. Having visited Jose several times at his home in Brixton, South London, I soon became more aware of the red stick methods. Guro Jose was a well-versed practitioner of the arts, having studies for years in Tapardo (long stick), Rat Irada (the retreating style), Bali Tok and De Campo (Largo Mano). He was to prove to be my 'Morpheus of the matrix'. I asked him to define the tourist version of Eskrima; he laughed and replied, "I don't really know since I've never been on holiday to the Philippines." After twelve months of intensive training, Guro Jose informed me that he could no longer teach me and I was to be approached by two new teachers of my own ilk. Although quite saddened by this news, I took him at his word and returned home to Huddersfield where, within twelve days, both Andy Norman of Keysi Fighting Methods and then JKD man, Karl Tanswell, arrived at my academy on the very same day. Karl spent years polishing my trapping skills and stick and dagger movement then later introduced me to Matt Thornton's SMAC programme, whereas Andy Norman's influence and guidance has enabled me to totally recontextualise the Filipino arts as a whole.

Tony and Bob Sykes pictured with Karl Tanswell of JKD and straight Blast Fame

My influences include Krishna Godhania who put the Punio into Punio Sumbrada, Mark Deny of the Dog Brothers with his trademark 'higher consciousness through harder contact', Grand Master Abner Pasa, who reduced a former World Champion's ability to that of a raw beginner Jeet Kune Do's Bob Breen (who I will always consider to be the godfather of British Kali and Eskrima) and last but not least, Matt Thornton for his easy to learn SMAC (Stick fighting Methods and Counters) program.

All have proved instrumental in my understanding of Eskrima, Kali and Arnis. Together they've helped me reach the realisation of the paradox – that it's all complexly simple.

Study a system, yes, but don't become solely dependent on it. In other words, let the system serve you and not you the system. Take time to look outside the box pattern and see what's really going on. Thank you Guro Jose Bernado, I have not forgotten.

Disarm, Datarm, the drills unfold
Techniques borrowed, secrets sold
From the barking dogs, to the laughing cat,
We danced to the beat of the tapi tapi rap.

Guro Krishna Godhania looks on while our author (right) enjoys a padded stickfighting event

UK Eskrima History

1972 Remy Latosa (US airman) arrives in the UK.

1972 – 1974 Remy begins to train Wing Chun with Brian Jones. Brian realises Remy's skill and asks him to teach Eskrima. Remy teaches a mixture of Serrada, Cadena de Mano and Largo Mano. This is renamed Latosa Eskrima and the Philippine Martial Arts Society (PMAS) was formed. Notables to come out of this group were Bill Newman, Jay Dobrin and Steve Tappin. Newman was to work more closely with Latosa, taking him to Germany and working with Leung Ting and the Ving Tsun group.

1976c Latosa is featured in 'Fighting Arts International'. The first time FMA is featured in a British martial arts magazine.

1977c Bob Breen meets Jay Dobrin. Dobrin was installing a telephone in Bob's house. Bob begins training in the Latosa system under Dobrin. Bob's training partner is Ralph Jones.

1979 Breen invites Dan Inosanto to England to teach the first JKD / FMA seminars in the UK. At these seminars are Jones, Terry Barnett, John Harvey and Rick Young.

1980 Dan returns and continues to return most years to the present day.

1982 Jose Bernado arrives in the UK.

1984 Cass Magda and Chris Kent teach in the UK for the first time. Pat O'Malley starts training at Bob Breen's academy.

1986 Larry Hartsell teaches first seminars in the UK.

1987 Seminar explosion begins by Hartsell, Magda, Kent, Inosanto and others Andy Gibney begins training in JKD / FMA with Terry Barnett.

The first World Instructor Conference is held in Cebu City in the Philippines The English contingent includes Bob Breen and Simon Wells. Simon is made an instructor in Lapunti Arnis de Abanico; he is the first English man to do so.

1989 The World Eskrima Arnis Kali Foundation (WEAKF) is formed.
The first World Championships are held in Cebu City.
The first English man to win a world title is Gary Derrick (Light Heavyweight).
The 6 members of the first British team are John Harvey, Bob Breen, Simon Wells, Gordon McAdam, Simon Burgess and Gary Derrick.

1990 Diony Canete teaches Doce Pares in the UK for the first time. This is another coup for Bob Breen.
The first British stick fighting Championships are held in the UK.
Richard Bustillo teaches for the first time in the UK. Brought to the UK by John Carrigan and Martin Sterling.

1991 Pep Padovano, Richard Hudson and Tony Jones are the first English martial artists to study Doce Pares in the Philippines.
Mike Inay (Inayan System) is brought to the UK by Bob Breen.

1992 The second World Championships are held in the Philippines. Tony Agostini and Pat O'Malley are crowned World Champions. Other team members are Krishna Godhania, Andy Gibney, John Harvey and Lee Banda. The coach is Bob Breen.
Abner Pasa (Warriors system) first comes to the UK. Krishna Godhania becomes his representative.

1993 The first European Championships are held in London. Bob Breen retires from coaching and passes his mantle to John Harvey and Pat O'Malley.
Rapid Arnis is formed by John Harvey and Pat O'Malley.

1994 The third World Championships are held in the Philippines. World Champions are John Harvey, Rezar Rahman and Andy Nugent. This is the largest team yet (21 members). The first woman to compete for the UK is Gabi Best. WEKAF (GB) is formed.

1995 The second European Championships are held in Ballymena Northern Ireland. The first female World Champions are Donna Ibbott and Anne-Marie Wright.
The first UK seminars for Danny Guba and Percival Pableo (Doce Pares) are held. Mark Marshall, British Team member, brings them to the UK.

1996 The fourth World Championships are the first held outside of the Philippines in Los Angeles produces the first GB female World Champions – Cindy McGrath, Anne-Marie Wright and Donna Ibbot. Other World Champions are John Harvey, Matt Twigg and Neil McLeod.
A major split in WEKAF (GB) occurs, principal members Andy Gibney, Anne-Marie Wright and Mark Hayes leave to form the British Eskrima Federation. This folds in 2002.
Danny Guba and Percival Pableo (Doce Pares) move to the UK. Percival goes back to the Philippines in 1997; Danny remains in the UK and begins the spread of Doce Pares in the UK.

1997 The BEF league begins a series of Eskrima tournaments consisting of 6 events. This runs for three years meaning that there were events for both WEKAF (GB) and the BEF during this time period.

1998 The first UK seminar appearance by Grandmaster Cacoy Canete (Doce Pares 12th Dan) the worlds highest graded Eskrima Master.

1999 Jose Bernado holds his first UK seminar. The first UK Doce Pares Conference by Grandmaster Cacoy Canete, Grandmaster Richard Bustillo, Danny Guba and Andy Gibney. There are over 100 participants.

2000 + A greater diversity of FMA in the UK grows as the UK becomes a hotbed for different styles. There are now Kapatiran Arnis, Modern Arnis, Kali Illustrismo, Sayoc Kali, Balintawak and Rapid Arnis as well as the established styles of the Inosanto blend and Doce Pares.
In 2001 Andy Gibney took a British Team to the first Doce Pares World Championships where they became World Champions.
The WEKAF World Championships are held every two years with the 2002 event being held in London under the stewardship of John Harvey, John James and Jude Tucker. There are also low armour contests after the formation of the Black Eagle Society in 1996.

2005 Grandmaster Jose Bernado dies.

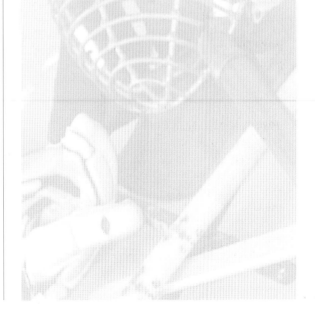

Techniques of Eskrima

Eskrima made easy with systemised Eskrima's Tony and Bob Sykes.

Fig. 1.1 **Fighters ready**

Fig. 1.2 **Under cover of a roof block white attempts...**

Fig. 1.3
An angle one attack, blue anticipates this motion and...

Fig. 1.4 **Responds with a well timed thrusting technique**

Fig. 1.5 **Then by stepping in blue simply clears the way for a...**

Fig. 1.6 **Well placed strike to white's eye**

Fig. 2.1 *Fighters ready*

Fig. 2.2 *White avoiding blue's 'live hand',
white moves in and traps blue's stick*

Fig. 2.3 **Painfully peels blue's thumb**

Fig. 2.4 *And it's one in the eye for blue*

Fig. 2.5 Methods such as these always make disarms that little bit more effective

Fig. 3.1
***Exponents of the South
East Asian martial arts
prepare for battle***

Fig. 3.2 ***Blue moves in...***

Fig. 3.3 And strikes across the face

Fig. 3.4 *Blue drops low*

Fig. 3.5 *Then drops white with a popular take down*

*Fig. 3.6 **This spells the end of white's Eskrima career***

Fig. 4.1
Blue attacks, white defends

Fig. 4.2 **White switches the angle**

Fig. 4.3
Changing the line,
white takes control and...

Fig. 4.4 **Smashes blue's hand**

Fig. 4.5 *Following the motion white takes out blue with a deadly thrust*

Fig. 4.6 *And prepares*

Fig. 4.7, Fig. 4.8 and Fig. 4.9
A rather common Filipino finish

The *Learning Never Stops*

While in pursuit of further enlightenment, I found myself stumbling across and at times even indulging myself in many great martial arts systems

The Keysi fighting method for example, was introduced to me by Andy Norman, the UK representative for the style. Its founder from Spain, Justo Dieguez first formed this revolutionary method when he became disillusioned with the sporting aspects of martial arts. He had come to realise that the reality of fighting meant NO RULES. Having now worked on and off with Andy Norman since 1999, I came to know Keysi fighting as a true martial art, one which has not compromised itself to fit into a sporting format but rather a modern method designed to fit well into the 21st century. Built on instinct and reaction, its application, is 100% real and is a suitable expansion for former freestylers who are perhaps searching for non-traditional pastime.

These days I consider myself to be a very lucky man. Mainly because, from time to time, I get chance to train one to one with the likes of Rick Young. Rick is a student under Guru Dan Inosanto - credentials enough, anyone might think. However Rick is a rare breed of man, one who studies each system he approaches in a more than diligent manner. His skill and ability are matched only by his modesty but when it comes to Jeet Kune Do, Judo, Brazilian Jui Jitsu, Boxing and may more, he is, without doubt, a world class player.

More recently, no holds barred and mixed martial arts have begun to impact onto the scene. Even while this was becoming all the rage and every man and his dog appeared to be jumping on the bandwagon, I recall being far more impressed by the more traditionally based methods such as Indonesian Pencak Silat.

Bob pictured with the respected Alvin Guinanao of Walisongo Pencak Silat.

Our author meets Rick Money Maker and other "Players to the Game".

In my quest to continue training and developing in different areas, fortune smiled on me recently when an old Kickboxing associate, Lance Lewis, relocated to my home town of Huddersfield, thanks to his job as a school inspector. Anyone who has followed Lance's achievements will be aware of his unparalleled reputation. He first began his full contact Kickboxing careers at the youthful age of 15. This was during the mid seventies, an era when the only opponents on offer were adult black belts. However, this didn't prove to be a barrier for Lance and he prevailed in becoming British Kickboxing Champion at the ripe old age of 16 and a year later went on to defeat the world WAKO champion.

Bob Sykes and friends 2002. Left to Right
Karl Tanswell, Peter Constadine, Bob Sykes, Erik Paulson, Clive Elliot, Geoff Thompson, Rick Young.
Kneeling ~ Christina Norman and Andy Norman.

From there he went on to box professionally and rapidly rose to the top, ranked number 3 in the UK and number 9 in Europe.

He was also a member of the now famous Kronk boxing team along with great fighters such as Thomas Hearns, Milton McRory, Lindell Holmes and Hector Camacho. Some may recall Lance making national news during the eighties when, after receiving a six year ban from boxing, he took on the assumed name Tony Dore and actually fought twelve further professional bouts. It's qualities such as these that make Lance a one off. When they forged this square ring combatant they most certainly disposed of the mould!

Lance has always maintained that martial arts are responsible for giving him the discipline to understand his own intelligence, which has led to him achieving an honours degree and undertaking a PhD.

The martial arts, particularly Tai Chi (which Lance has now practiced for over twenty years) have maintained his physique and helped him gate back in touch with his physical abilities. Lance often talks about the idea of life being a lot more than we are led to believe and that we should always check out what might be as well as what definitely is.

The hard-hitting Peter Consterdine of the BCA once referred to Lance's blend of Tai Chi as "Tai Chi with issues". Perhaps he's got a point. I've been reduced to tears on more than one occasion both during and after a Lance Lewis Tai chi workshop.

Nevertheless, the ability to dig deep is another quality of Lance that I admire, along with his obvious transcendence of grade, rank, titles, past glories and to some extent his more effective physical abilities.

To cut to the chase, Lance's quest is to help people reveal themselves to themselves, this is an area I suspect that most martial artists prefer to overlook, especially in a world where the vast majority of martial artists are free to delude themselves to the highest degree.

As well as linking the many different Western boxing fighting styles to the breath control of Tai Chi, both Lance and myself are keen students of Pencak Silat Wali Songo as taught by Pendekar Steve Benitez.

We are both very interested in how this remarkable lineage has remained so untainted throughout the years and just how well every principle-based shape links to the next.

Although Lance has now been teaching me his many styles of boxing for over two years, the elements of Tai Chi and Pencak Silat Wali Songo have begun to creep in and mainly dominate much of the training session. A normal day usually consists of about twenty minutes Silat followed by boxing. This normally takes the shape of moving around playing a sort of tig game and concentrating on the breath by letting go of the technique in hand! Lucky for me, Lance has been very kind in imparting to me a few of the secrets which made him such an awesome combatant, many of which pay dividends during my weekly sparring sessions with the renowned Huddersfield boxer, Richard Sykes.

More often than not we finish our session with around ten to fifteen minutes of Tai Chi, which my chief instructor Steve Rowe will be pleased to hear, is fast becoming a very significant aspect of the overall picture. Having said that, it's not all been plain sailing, especially for old "has-beens" such as myself. Perhaps there's a grain of truth in what people suggest when they refer to the majority of martial arts instructors as having difficulty in receiving information.

It's as though our dials seem to have inadvertently got themselves stuck onto transmitting mode only.

Out of the vast amount of people I've both met and talked with, the lion's share have indicated to me their sincere desire to break the mould and take on new material. However, as they themselves put it, the comfort and security of a less hazardous swim in their own ponds keep luring them back. Their words, not mine! And who can really blame them, to take on new systems and shed old skins takes time, effort and the occasional sacrifice. Nonetheless, it's evidently become a great way for battle-scarred veterans such as Lance and myself to fill that ever-expanding void.

Bob with long term sparring partner Richard Sykes

"Happy Days," Bob practicing Walisongo Silat with his son and hero Oliver.

What About Bob?
By those who know him best!

Geoff Thompson

Fighter Writer

Bob Sykes always steps up to the plate.
Whether it is fighting world champions
in the ring, offering his opinion without
fear of favour or otherwise, or
pioneering the best martial arts
magazine in Britain today he can
always be relied upon to deliver when
others are on the side -lines talking
the good fight. I love Bob Sykes
because his word, his integrity and
his martial arts are all world class.

James Sinclair

United Kingdom
Wing Chun Kung Fu Association.

Bob hates politics and ego, this makes

him a great ambassador for the martial

arts. He prefers to train than talk, and

comes at you from that angle. He has

an uncanny ability to disarm you and

get straight to the point.

He is a Yorkshireman!

Lance Lewis
World Kickboxing Champion.

I first consciously recall meeting Bob when I refereed one of his fights in Liverpool 1985. During that fight, I recall him doing a jumping spinning back kick and catching his opponent somewhere in the stomach. Oh! I thought that was juicy.

The next time we met was in 1988 at the Bill Wallace seminar in Manchester. Here I sparred with Bob and found him a tough cookie, who moved in a one-dimensional plane, where as I had been trained to move three dimensionally in the ring. I therefore found the gaps he left easy to exploit and managed to avoid his spinning back kick. The next time I recall was Bob talking about him to Danny Conners, Bob had a way of winding Danny up, this was usually through a range of wit, sarcasm and as both were schooled in verbal warfare once they both got together it was like watching another kind of martial arts, head and tongue style. During the final stages of my fight career, David Berry radically overhauled my training programme. Therefore, for my last two world title fights, Dave brought me up to the Colne Valley Black Belt Academy in Huddersfield, West Yorkshire. Bob's dojo where he, Buster Reeves and Richard Sykes acted as sparring partners.

It was here that Bob and I started to talk a lot together, especially about the social issues affecting young people. Once I won the world title in '97 I wanted nothing to do with anything that looked like training or the martial arts, with the exception of practising Tai Chi and Qi Gung on my own.

However, in 1999 I moved to Huddersfield, West Yorkshire, to start my job a a school inspector. I visited Bob's dojo and sure enough in a short matter of time he had me training (lightly, no more heavy stuff thanks, we both agree that we both physically tortured our bodies for long enough). Coaching, learning and very occasionally sparring. During our twice-weekly training, Bob gently encouraged me to unpack, articulate and then coach a vast amount of high level boxing training and coaching that I have received over the years, and then he showed belief and confidence in me by having me coach one of his super seminar events. Through Bob, I started to learn Pencak Silat Wali Songo and he remains my role model in this.

In a way Bob and his team have acted like uncles to my sons, teaching and coaching them and been role models around them.
Having become good friends with Bob now, I see how he was able to wind Danny Conners up, in my eyes he has taken over Danny's role, in my life and the martial arts. The ego buster. And through Bob just like Danny, I have met many wonderful Martial Artists. *A true martial Warrior, Nuff Respects.*

Joe Tierney
Captain of the Warriors.

I met Bob around 1982 at a quest for champions at the time I was British Light Weight Chaampion. He complemented me on my fighting ability, which helped fuel my inflated "young ego" I had in those days. Next time I met him was in a fight off for third place. It was a hard fight which I won but I think the decision was a bit on the dubious side towards myself. I did not hear from him again or see him until the late 80's when he phoned me and asked if I remembered him and he went on to say he was editor of a new magazine, which he wanted me to feature in. Never one to look a gift horse in the mouth I travelled to Huddersfield and developed a friendship which would change my life. My friendship with Bob took me on a journey in which I encountered knowledge, hardship, elation, brotherhood, kinship and a career. To say he had an influence in my life is an understatement. He provided me with opportunities that I probably would not have come across if I had not befriended him.

The ultimate accolade Bob bestowed on me was to be his best man at his wedding. That was a bond of true friendship and honour. I could write a book on Bob and our exploits but to sum him up *I would say he is one of the most talented, knowledgeable, witty and influential martial artists of our time.*

Pendekar Steven Benitez

Bob is a student of the Walisongo Pencak Silat system and actually teaches several classes a week at his huge Colne Valley Black Belt Academy. Bob is one of the easiest going people I know with a huge sense of humour and is a real practical joker. Someone in his esteemed position could well let that fame and power go to their heads but I must say, Bob has been fantastic, allowing me to be creative in his articles I write for his magazine as well as regularly hosting us for seminars. Bob came through as a fighter of great reputation in the same era as stars like Alfie Lewis, Kevin Brewerton and others. He is a great example of how a completely different change of direction martial arts-wise can re-ignite passion.

Kickboxing and Silat are poles apart and yet with his consistency and dogged determination he is making progress as a Silat player.

A special thankyou for those who have helped me along the way!

Karate Do.

John Baxter 1st Dan. My first instructor and mentor

John Wright 2nd Dan. The true meaning of contact

Phillip Robinson 2nd Dan. Hard physical training

Donnie Wray 1st Dan. Hard sparring sessions

Niel Kane 1st Dan. Encouragement

Dave Coats 6th Kyu. My first head kick

Ticky Donovan 8th Dan. For my black belt

Steve Rowe 7th Dan. For his guidance

Phil Milner 10th Dan. For setting a fine example

Dave Allen 10th Dan. He made my life hell

Russell Stutely 7th Dan. For introducing me to pressure points

Jon Jepson 6th Dan. For his trust

Kickboxing

Tom Gunning. My first boxing coach

Phil Mayo. Thanks for the opportunity

Arthur O'Loughlin. Thanks for the humour

Phil Glover. Another great sense of humour

Lance Lewis. For teaching me to move

Richard Sykes. Twenty years of sparring

Master Woody. For cornering my first Thai bout

Ronnie Green. A good friend

Kung Fu

Master Michael Lee. Who took the forms title where as I won the fighting!

Master Danny Khalid. For fixing my knee

George Wellington. My first kung fu instructor

James Sinclair. For being himself

Master Derek Jones. Good memories

Taekwondo

Master Shin. Hard Saturday afternoon sessions in 1983

Patrick Duggan. For getting me started in 1977

Jackson White (TAGB). For a couple of hard fights

Master Frank Murphy. For his guidance

Eskrima and Jeet Kune Do

John Harvey. First disarm

Pat O'Malley. Second disarm

Jude Tucker. Third disarm

Bob Breen. Helping me understand Hubud

Karl Tanswell. Stick and dagger

Rick Young. Far better stick and dagger

Andy Norman. Total extreme stick and dagger

Abna Pasa. More Hubud

Danny Guba. Helping me get my stick moving

Jose Bernardo. Showing me the way!

Pencak Silat

Abdul Jahoor. The world's best instructor

Steve Benitez. Great example of live silat

Alvin Guinanao. Great movement

Jak Othman. A true master

Master Yeop. A really nice person

Chris Parker. Strange but true

Martine Lopez. A true Christian

Judo

Gareth Howell. Who also designed this book.

Bob Wilson. The wise old judoka

The Warriors Squad

Joe Tierney	*Peter O'Para*
Chris Williams	*Dave Craydon*
Neil Williams	*Chris Boughey*
Phil Prout	*Ed Burn*
David Rowland	*Tom Wynne*
Buster Reeves	*Keith Priestley*
John Dawson	*Tony Sykes*
Corney Wiley	*Mark Jundy*
Billy Bryce	*Ivor Priest*
Billy Priest	*Karl Priest*
Graham Abdulla	*Shabier Ahktar*
Paul Marsden